Jump, Kit, jump.
Jump with Bill.
I will sit
with baby Jill.

1

Jump, Kit, jump,
with a one and a two.

Jump, Kit, jump.
It is time for you.

Jump, Bill, jump.
It is time for you.

Jump with Kit.
It is time for two.

Jump, Jill, jump.
All three will fit.

But Jill will NOT jump
with Bill and Kit!

Jump, Jill, jump.
And WE will sit!